Jimmy Sloman

May You Be Happy

OceanBlue Publishing
Tiburon, CA

1st edition

Any OceanBlue product,
including this book, can be
ordered 24 hours a day:

(800) 852-4890

(707) 838-6200
(abroad, 9-5 PST)

www.ocean-blue.com
(site available Feb '99)

OceanBlue Publishing
98 Main Street
Tiburon, CA 94920

CONTENTS

PART 1
Heart

CHAPTER 1

LETTING BE

Hello to you!
Here's the deal, as far as I can tell:

We all want to be happy. And we are sometimes. But then other times we're not. And when we're not, we wonder, why aren't we happy all the time? Why does there have to be suffering?

Some very great beings have pondered that very question, including Jesus and the Buddha and Lao-Tzu and the Dalai Lama and Ramana Maharshi and Byron Katie and many others.

It seems that each of these people made a discovery and they were trying to communicate about what they discovered. I think they each basically discovered the same thing, but because they were different people living at different times in different societies it all came out sounding different.

Here's what I sense they discovered:

That all of our suffering arises from our disagreements with Reality.

Now right away an objection arises, which is one I had myself for a long time. And it's this:

If I don't have some resistance to the way things are, then how can anything ever improve?

But maybe a different metaphor is called for:

Imagine that you're a gardener, and you've planted a seed in the ground. Now is there anything wrong with that seed? No, of course not. It's perfect just the way it is. Nevertheless, there's a place for watering it, for nurturing it each day.

Maybe this world is like that. Maybe it's perfect just the way it is—and there's a place for nurturing it, too.

"Resist not evil," Jesus said. The "evil" part is a mistranslation, I believe. What he really meant, in my opinion, was to let go of our contractions around any part of this existence that we find unacceptable.

Why? Because to the extent that we resist anything or anybody being the way they are, we're going to hurt. We're going to suffer.

But then how will anything change?

Paradoxically, when we can let go inside of our need

for anything or anybody to be different than they are, things change on their own in a mysterious way.

Because now we're nurturing that seed with love. And that perfect seed tends to grow into something else equally perfect, maybe a beautiful apple tree. It's perfect all the way through the process.

Maybe the world is that way.

My friend Byron Katie says that she's simply stopped arguing with Reality. Because she noticed that everytime she did, she felt disconnected, fearful or whatever. She didn't feel good.

And she noticed that whenever she's not arguing with Reality, she automatically feels good. Why not? Maybe we were meant to feel good and in tune. Maybe that's our natural state.

And what prevents us from being in our natural state? Maybe it's our ideas about how the world or this person or that situation or whatever should be different.

Sosan, the third patriarch of Zen, put it this way:

"The great Way is not difficult; only cease to cherish your opinions."

I don't know about you, but I notice that my mind has all kinds of stories about how things ought to be in the future, how they should have been in the past, and so on and so forth.

Apparently that's what minds do. They make up stories about how things should be or should have been, or how they ought to change or be different somehow. Or how somebody—yes, maybe even ourselves—ought to change or be different.

But as far as I can tell, everything in this Existence can't help being the way it is. It just is that way.

Can you help being the way you are? No, of course not. You're just that way. Maybe tomorrow you'll be different in some way, but right now you can't help being the way you are.

But here's the interesting thing. When somebody loves you exactly the way you are, you tend to blossom. You tend to grow. You tend to flower.

You may even leave behind some old "negative" patterns based on anger or fear or feeling hurt in some way. Some kind of contraction that you had.

But notice that it's the people who love and accept you just the way you are, who have no resistance to the way you are right now, who allow you to blossom into something more expanded.

Conversely—check this out for yourself—when you're around somebody who's got a problem with you, who feels that there's something wrong with you, who feels that you need to be "fixed" in some way, don't you tighten up? Resist them? Not much blossoming there.

Love is what makes the difference. The willingness to let go of all the resistance to the way things are. And paradoxically, then they get to be different. Then that perfect seed gets to blossom into a more mature kind of existence.

Everybody I mentioned earlier, and lots of other folks that I didn't mention, mainly people we tend to think of as spiritual masters of one sort or another—here's what I think happened to them:

They fell in love with Existence.

Exactly as it is. Right down to the last grain of sand. They let go of all their stories about how it ought to be, and all their resistances to how it is.

And as soon as they did that, all their suffering stopped. Because there was no resistance anymore to cause any suffering. Then they could just hang out with this beautiful Existence and love it the way it is.

It's that very love that waters the seed and allows it to grow into something more evolved.

CHAPTER 2

LIGHT

"Hatred never ceases by hatred. Hatred only ceases by love," the Buddha said.

Picture yourself facing a large dragon. This dragon can represent anybody or anything that you have resistance to or about deep down. Deep down, we feel they or it should be different.

And we have a story about this dragon. This dragon is wrong, should not have done what they did, should not be the way they are, should not have treated me or us or my nation or my religion or my sex or whatever that way.

Whatever happened should not have happened. It was wrong to have happened that way. It shouldn't be that way now. It or they are wrong.

This is our suffering.

The Buddha said that all suffering is caused by attachment. Attachment to what? To our stories, concepts, ideas, beliefs, to the very things that we know to be most "true."

I notice that my mind has a story about everything and everybody. Some are "good," some are "bad."

I notice that my mind makes judgments about everything. This is good, that is bad, this is beautiful, that is ugly, this is right, that is wrong, this is desirable, that is not desirable.

On and on, judging. Comparing. Deciding what's right and what's wrong. And condemning the "wrong."

The master Osho suggested a beautiful metaphor:

Picture yourself being in a darkened room. And imagine that you're walking around and you're stumbling over the furniture, because you can't see. Now you can fight with that furniture, with that darkness. But fighting with darkness becomes exhausting because darkness basically doesn't exist; it's just an absence of light.

Once you turn on the light, the problem of stumbling over the furniture disappears immediately because now you can see. The problem disappears as a by-product of more light being in the situation. You don't need to "defeat" the furniture.

Our problems are like this. When we relax into letting things be the way they are, into being friends with

Existence, something miraculous happens. That little seed of beauty that was there starts growing now.

For instance, suppose we're having a problem with someone. We don't like the way they've behaved. We're irritated, disappointed or fearful of them.

Now suppose we were to just let go of our story about how they ought to be. We just relax it, like letting a closed fist open.

What then? Do we let that person walk all over us? Do we take back the person we broke up with? Do we let somebody who's harming us continue to do so? Do we keep putting up with this behavior pattern?

No, it doesn't mean that. But what we'll do can't be predicted either, because now our acts won't come from a rule or a story; they'll come from a different perspective. What we do will look like whatever it looks like, but now it will come from our intuitive heart guidance, the guidance that operates below the realm of stories and tends to produce more harmonious and magical results.

Conversely, asking "negative" types of questions—What's wrong with this person? situation? world? etc.—tends not to lead to the best kinds of outcomes, because they focus our attention on what we don't want or like, thus actually reinforcing it.

However we answer or deal with such questions, we're still putting our attention on what's wrong and thus "growing" that.

Because wherever we put our attention flourishes and grows in our life. Whatever we put our thought and feeling on becomes more real for us, and then we have to deal with it more often.

Peter Drucker, the management guru, advised businesses to "starve the problem, feed the opportunity."

Not that we ignore the problem, whatever it is, but that we start transferring more of our attention to whatever opportunity exists in the situation.

How do we find that opportunity? Tony Robbins, the neurolinguistic mentor, advises asking ourselves questions to direct our attention. Questions such as:

What am I happy about?

What am I proud of?

What am I grateful for?

What am I committed to?

Asking such questions shifts our attention to something more fruitful.

He then advises addressing the problem itself and asking questions such as these:

What's great about this?

How can I use this?

It's a way of focusing attention on the opportunity. And then the opportunity grows, because we've changed the agenda. We're putting our attention on something new, the opportunity, and that grows instead.

Let's take an example.

When I was a boy my father decided it would save electricity if the lights were turned out whenever we left a room. So he suggested to me that I do that. And here's what happened:

When I did turn out the lights, it was ignored. It was expected. But when I didn't, my Dad would remind me that I hadn't turned out the lights, sometimes with increasing irritation that I wasn't "getting it."

My father had a very good heart and his intention was well-meaning. But he didn't understand the principle involved, and neither did I.

Rationally, that approach makes sense, doesn't it? You tell someone what they're doing wrong, as often as necessary, and then they correct it and do the "right" thing instead.

Unfortunately, it doesn't work very well that way. In this example, because I was frequently being negatively reinforced and almost never positively reinforced, I never did learn to turn out the lights when leaving a room.

I would make resolutions about it, I would try my best, but I still failed to do it again and again. And each time it was pointed out to me. I was a "failure" at it. Because of that and similar issues, the relationship between my Dad and I fared poorly as well.

It took me about 45-50 years of life to really begin to understand the simple principle that my father could have used. All he needed to do was the exact opposite—

that is, appreciate me when I did turn out the lights and just ignore it when I didn't.

Then he would have been feeding the opportunity, starving the problem. He would have been watering—with his attention—what he did want rather than what he didn't. The results would have been vastly different.

One time I watched a father push his daughter on a swing. And what I noticed that day was this: That he always pushed the swing in the direction it was already going. When the swing was going the "opposite" way, the father just ignored that. Then when the swing was going in the "fruitful" direction again, the father would reinforce that.

When I got my cat Nicky about eight years ago, he was really a handful. Apparently he had been misused by his previous owners, because if you got within about four feet of him he would put up his claws and bare his fangs and hiss and spit. He was a pretty scared and angry and neurotic cat.

Anyway, when he did that I would just ignore it. I would just go about my business and leave him alone. But whenever he would let me get a little bit closer to him, perhaps by accident, I would give him a little snack immediately.

As time went on and he let me pet him, I would pet him and show him I loved him as much as possible, and just ignore any hostile behavior.

What happened is that he eventually relaxed and turned into this beautiful animal with a wonderful personality. He still has a bit of an "edge" to him until he gets to know somebody, but once he gets to know them a little bit, he's a relaxed, affectionate, great cat. He's enjoying his life.

By appreciating the beautiful Being latent in Nicky and reinforcing that, he became more of his natural self. We all have that beautiful Being inside of us because we all partake of Existence.

When we look for the beautiful seed in any situation and water that with our attention and our love, then that seed starts to grow into its natural potential, which is harmony, love, joy, creativity, spontaneity, and so on—the natural Self of the situation or person.

CHAPTER 3

NURTURING

How do we find that Self or that natural seed of the situation? We look for it. As Jesus said, we get what we ask for, we find what we're looking for. So we have the intention to find it.

And then we "jump out of the system," as hakomi founder Ron Kurtz advised. We look at it all in a new way that doesn't remain boxed in by the old way.

Perhaps the most fundamental way to do that, to shift our perspective in a situation, is to begin to release the stories we have about it, to release our resistance to whatever is there, to cease to continue our argument with Reality.

Imagine that you're standing in a mighty river and trying to walk upstream. The river seems to relentlessly battle you; it just won't stop pounding you and pushing against you.

Sometimes our lives can feel like that.

But notice that the river has nothing against you; it's just going the way it's going.

It's not the river's job—Existence's job—to get in accord with us; it's vast and we're an atom. Rather, it's our job to get in accord with it—by letting go, by turning around and letting it carry us.

When we're floating down the river, when we've let go of our resistance to it, our sight improves. We're not so preoccupied by the struggle, and we can see things that we couldn't have seen otherwise. We can see opportunities perhaps, or our energy can move in ways that it could not have done before.

But what about giving correction then? Is it ever appropriate? Aren't there times, for instance, when the arithmetic teacher must show her student the mistake he's making in doing fractions?

Yes. But it's worth mentioning a very interesting study that was done concerning teachers and students. What the researchers measured was the ratio of "positive" to "negative" feedback that the teacher was giving to each student and to the class in general. And what they found was this:

The teacher needed to create a positive context for each student before correcting them.

Specifically, teachers had to make at least three-quarters of their comments "positive," telling the student what she was doing right, what was good about her work, and so on. When the teachers did that, the students were very motivated and did well.

However, if the "negative"—corrective—comments to the students increased above one-quarter of all comments the students lost motivation, became apathetic or rebellious, and did poorly.

In any situation, then, we want to be as patient as possible and whenever possible wait until we can push the swing in the direction it's already going, in the "fruitful" or "nurturing" direction.

Then we're watering and nurturing the seed of what we do want. We're turning on a light instead of trying to fight the darkness.

Let's take another example, one from Ken Keyes: Suppose the cook's putting too much salt in the soup. So we mention that. Now either the cook is going to say that he didn't realize that and he cuts down the salt, or he defends his "position." In the face of that, it's futile to keep pointing out the "error" to him. Then he would just set his heels in self-righteousness about his position.

The first thing we can do is drop our resistance to the situation. Maybe we eat a little less soup or skip the soup part of the meal. We let go of our attachment that the soup has to be a certain way. We relax and let Reality be the way it is.

But sooner or later the soup will be a bit less salty, perhaps by accident. Then we naturally respond with our pleasure and appreciation. "You know, I noticed the soup was a little less salty today. It tasted really good. Thank you for that."

And this is not just about salty soup. During the Cuban missle crisis, President Kennedy received a threatening and bellicose message from Chairman Khruschev. Then, some hours later, he received a more conciliatory message. No one knew what to do.

It was JFK's brother Bobby who suggested the solution: Ignore the first message; respond to the second.

This approach takes more patience, but it has one great advantage—it works like crazy. And it supports relationships, too, rather than alienating them.

Researchers did a study of couples, and they found that they could predict who would stay together and who would break apart from just one kind of observation: The ratio of positive to negative comments that they said to each other.

The couples that stayed together, on average, said five times as many positive as negative comments to each other. On the other hand, the couples that broke apart, on average, said one-and-a-half times as many negative as positive comments to each other. That one thing could predict the outcome.

What we give attention to expands.

What we nourish, with our attention, grows.

Let's now go back to the dragon. What would be the most fundamental way of dealing with it?

Well, suppose we "woke up" and discovered that our fight with the dragon was in a dream? Upon waking up from the dream, the problem would simply dissolve. It would become irrelevant, like our childhood toys left in the closet and no longer used. It's not that anything was "wrong" with our childhood toys; it's just that we move on to other things.

That is about what happens when we let go of our stories about the world, ourselves, and other people, and how it, we, or them are supposed to be better or different in some way.

From that letting-go place, we can then nurture the situation in ways that we couldn't have done before. Then the beautiful, natural seed latent in the situation will tend to begin evolving even though we're not trying to "improve" anybody or anything anymore.

Then, replacing our desiring of this or that, we're "inspired" to act in some way. Our inner energy will move in some direction concerning the situation, perhaps, but without our clinging to or craving about some particular outcome.

All of this doesn't mean that we can't set boundaries if that's appropriate; it doesn't mean that we always stay in every situation; it doesn't mean that we're necessarily passive. Indeed, it's possible that we may even need to be a warrior. The actions that will move from our inner heart and energy—behind all the stories—can't be predicted.

But they will tend to produce more harmonious and fruitful results, since we've let go of the compulsion that something or somebody needs to be different. We're able to appreciate this beautiful Reality just as it is, while it evolves in its own organic way.

CHAPTER 4

MIRRORING

When we do need to set a boundary of some kind, hopefully we can do so without putting anyone out of our heart. Why? For our own sake. When we're clinging to a story about how something or somebody should have been different in the past or should be different now, our heart hurts.

Check it out for yourself. Look inside and notice that anytime there's a judgment or condemnation about some aspect of Existence, there's a feeling of tightness and disconnection and contraction inside.

Jesus addressed this point. He talked about love a lot, and he talked about what makes unconditional love possible—non-judgmentalness. He talked about this in many ways:

"Judge not that ye be not judged."

"Let he who is without sin cast the first stone."

"Before you judge the speck in your brother's eye, look at the log in your own eye."

This approach is about letting go of our resistance to any part of Reality being the way it is. It's about falling in love with Existence just as it is.

Once again the mind jumps in and says, "But then how will this world ever be 'improved'?" Mysteriously, it's only when we've begun to fall in love with this world, and all aspects of the people and things in it, that we can truly begin to nurture that seed to a more mature state.

The seed doesn't get more perfect, but it does evolve into a more developed form, perhaps a tree or a blade of grass or a rose bush—when we "allow" it to, when we nurture it, when we drop our aversion to any part of Existence and open our heart to all of it instead.

And not coincidentally, we feel much better. We feel connected, whole, joyful.

It's a good test for whatever spiritual or other path we're following in life. If that path is resulting in more open-heartedness, it's probably a fruitful path for us. If it's not, then what's the point?

No matter how many great truths we're learning or how many peak experiences we're having, or how many "undesirable" things or people we're wiping out, is it leading to more love in our heart, more love in the world?

Because the world is just you and I multiplied a few billion times. If it doesn't start in your heart and mine, where will it start? And isn't a more loving world, a world where we can truly love each other, what we really want?

From a place of loving Existence as it is, we're far more able to potentially turn on a light instead of fighting with the darkness, nurturing that seed instead of trying to "improve" it from a place of fear, resentment or anger, which only leads to more of the same.

The world is basically a big mirror for us. What we see and experience "out there" is basically a reflection of what's going on inside us. We see what we're looking for, what we put our attention on.

The resistance we feel inside us to anything in this Existence is mirrored by our external experience. Why? Because it is our stories of the world and the beings in it that determines our experience of the world, and thus our actions in it. Our experience of the world also determines our vibration, and thus what we "magnetize" to us.

When we approach any part of the world from fear or anger—aversion—we're adding to the collective fear and anger in the world. And our actions tend to create more fear and anger and grief in ourselves and others.

Conversely, when we approach the world with love we're adding to the collective love in the world. How else can a world that loves itself come about except through you and me?

When we let go of our stories about what's "wrong" and about how whoever or whatever "should" be different, we're in a place of vastly greater possibilities.

Do we want the world to change? Let it begin with us inside. "As we change, the world changes," James Allen said. Each little bit of open-heartedness that we add inside leads to greater open-heartedness in the world, leads to that seed beginning to grow to its possibility.

That's why Jesus, when asked what was the greatest commandment, said that it was to love God and love our neighbor.

Those two are ultimately the same thing, because if we're not loving our neighbor yet we're not truly loving God either. Because God is our neighbor; God shows up as you and me and our neighbor and our "enemy" and the sky and the flowers in the field.

Imagine a wave on the ocean. Actually, the "wave" only exists within our mind. We look at some part of Existence and define it as something—"This is a wave."

But there's really only the Ocean, now showing up as this wave, now showing up as that wave. It's all just the Ocean, "waving." It's all just One Energy, One Source, showing up as you and me and everybody else and the stars and the mountains and the rivers. And the smiles and tears and the "beautiful" and the "ugly" and the "good" and the "bad"—all of it.

Lao-Tzu pointed out that things spring into existence in our mind as opposites. As soon as we form the concept of "up" we've also formed the concept of "down." "Up" literally has no meaning without the meaning of "down." They come into existence together.

So too with "long" and "short," "hot" and "cold," "day" and "night," "mountains" and "valleys." Can you have a mountain without a valley? No. As soon as a mountain is created, a valley is created at the same time. They go together.

Can we have sun without shadow? No. As soon as we step out into the sun, a shadow is created at the same time. If we want to eliminate all shadows we'd have to eliminate the sun as well. If we wanted to eliminate all "negativities" in Existence, we'd have to eliminate Existence itself.

Paradoxically, when we cease our argument with the "shadows" of Existence, the overall light in ourselves and in the world increases.

Then we do whatever we do, but from a different place. We may still work to save the environment, for example, but no longer from a place of fear or clutching or aversion or make-wrong.

Then we're more relaxed, and we do what we do to nurture the garden of this world without clinging to our stories about it and how it's supposed to turn out. And our hearts begin to fill with the unique internal joy that is the hallmark of unaddressed love.

Jesus emphasized the unaddressed nature of love. He said that if we just love those who love us, well, that's what everybody does. And if we're just good to those who are good to us, again it's not such a big deal because that's what we all do.

He said where our hearts really learn to open is when we can accept the "unacceptable," when we can love the "unlovable." He wanted us to see what the world looked like when we dropped our resistance to it.

He wanted us to see what the world looked like when we saw through all our stories about it.

We can't really know that even a single story is true. Stories are just stories. What exists is just Reality, beneath all the categories and beliefs, just as It is.

When we can love this world just as it is, with all of its horrors and beauties and tragedies and joys, then we're beginning to truly nurture that beautiful seed.

Just as you can't be any different in this moment, nothing else can either. Nothing can help being the way it is. As we begin to see this, we begin to forgive the world and ourselves and others for being what it and we are.

If you were born with the exact same genetic DNA as someone else, and you went through the exact same experiences they did, you'd probably have made the same decisions they did.

If you look back at your life, isn't it true that you've done the best you can? You or somebody else may think that parts of it weren't good enough, but weren't you always doing the best you knew how at that time?

Well everybody else is the same way. Everybody at all times is doing the best they know how to do at that moment. Even when the results are tragic, it was still the best that could be done at the time. If you or I or any other actor in the drama could have been more wise, more conscious, more mature in any given moment, we would have been.

It doesn't mean that we condone all actions. We still may need to set up appropriate boundaries of some kind. As Ken Keyes said, loving someone doesn't necessarily mean that we buy into their act.

What it means is just that we let go of our internal resistance to Reality being that way in that form.

It's almost as if Existence is playing Hide and Seek with us, and saying: "Can you love me like this? Can you love me like that? And what about this part of me?"

As Byron Katie says, how do we know that everything that happens is for the highest good? Because it happens. How do we know that the wind blowing is for the highest good? Because it's blowing.

CHAPTER 5

KINDNESS

There is immense suffering in this world. Even as we read or hear this, there are people in incredible pain in hospitals and elsewhere, there are people feeling lonely and isolated in prisons, there are people being tortured and violated and abused, there are animals suffering in "tight confinement" on factory farms.

Some people are starving, or watching their dreams starve. Some are feeling anxiety or terror or unbearable grief. Some are feeling hopeless or filled with hate. And there are many other forms of suffering in this world.

And there is the suffering in our own hearts. You know, that sense of "disjointedness" inside us that we carefully push down and ignore, but that is there if we really look?

This is not a Pollyanna view of life where the unpleasant and the painful are ignored or denied and only the "beautiful" is recognized. There is suffering in this world and in ourselves, along with joy.

The Buddha said that he taught one thing only: "Suffering and the end of suffering."

When we can move from seeing whatever-it-is as "wrong, evil, ugly, unfair" to "suffering and the end of suffering," we stop contributing to the suffering in the world and in ourselves—the suffering brought about by our resistance to some part of Existence.

Part of that resistance is our clinging to various things. We cling to people and places and things gone by. We cling to our beliefs and "truths" hoping they will make us a little more secure in this insecure world.

Our grasping, clutching, manipulating, the quality of insistence about what we want, is also part of our suffering. When we can drop our insistence about getting whatever, then we simply move however our inner energy moves us. And it results in whatever it results in. Existence is free to be more natural, more itself; it's free to begin blossoming to a new state of perfection.

Our ideas of how other people or the world or ourselves should be different is also part of our clinging. But again, no part of Existence can help being what it is. It was brought into Existence being that way, conditioned the way it was conditioned.

Everything expresses a unique part of Existence, and all of it is somehow necessary. "Night" must exist along with "day." "Winter" must exist with "summer." "Pain" must exist along with "pleasure." "Losing" must exist alongside "winning."

To eliminate all the "downs" and just have the "ups" would eliminate Existence itself, because it can't Exist except as all those dualities. As physicists tell us, when an electron comes into being, an anti-electron or positron always comes into existence at the same time. Dualities exist together.

When we can love it all as it is, our hearts open. Love shows up. God shows up here on earth, in you and in me.

If we want God to appear on earth, It has to show up in you and me. It has no other way to appear. God can only appear in your heart and my heart.

When our heart opens, then the divine shows up on earth. Because then we become a channel for divine love, which doesn't discriminate.

As Jesus points out, Existence sends its sun and its rain to saint and sinner alike. It doesn't ask who you are before it sends its warming sun to you. It doesn't ask who you are before it sends its healing rain to you.

And when the rain isn't healing, that's also part of Its healing rain. And when it's night and there's no light, that's also part of Its healing light. And when it's winter and cold, that's also part of Its healing warmth.

We can partake of that divine love when we are willing to love Existence as it is, just as it is, in all its multi-colored hues.

Then we let go of our grasping and clinging and aversion and judgments. Then joy enters our heart.

The Buddha gave us some advice to counteract the suffering of our wanting and clinging and clutching (and the opposite side of the same coin, our aversions). To put it in modern language, he advised reversing the direction of that flow 180 degrees.

He advised cultivating generosity. Generosity in our own heart—love. And generosity in an external sense, giving to the world however we can.

And he advised cultivating this, growing it just like a garden. He knew well that hearts don't grow overnight, but patiently, day by day, when an intention to nurture them exists.

When we're generous, we reverse the suffering of wanting and clinging. We're asking what we can give to this world rather than what we can take from it. We ask how we can nurture this person or this situation and help them or it to blossom rather than manipulating them or it to be different.

We partake of the joy of giving, then. As Francis of Assisi said, "Let me console rather than be consoled...for it is in giving that we receive."

When we can love this world and each other just as it and we are, in all our perfect imperfection, that is our greatest gift.

Where this greatest gift really shows up is in our everyday life. It shows up in how kindly we treat ourselves and each other and the world in our ordinary, day-to-day actions and encounters.

The Dalai Lama, when asked what his religion was, said: "My religion is kindness."

Is our spiritual path showing up as more everyday kindness, more open-heartedness and generosity in our ordinary life? Do we feel more in love with this world, with Existence?

Jesus was a person who loved Existence just as it was, and he wanted us to get a glimpse of what it was that he was seeing.

"Love one another as I have loved you," Jesus said to us.

And he gave us the Golden Rule, which can also be found in the Old Testament and in many other places and sources:

"Treat others in the way that you yourself would want to be treated."

When we can do that, or begin to, we begin to let go of this self-centered little clod of selfish interests and become a channel for something much vaster, not less than Everything.

Then we surrender our little life and our hidden-away misery and unhappiness and grasping and wanting and struggling, and let the energy of Existence move through us in whatever way It wants to.

We follow that inner energy, that inner guidance—which moves by itself and feels like love and possibility rather than fear—and find ourselves doing whatever it is we do without knowing why. There's no rhyme or reason anymore, it's all just happening by itself.

Notice your breathing. It was happening before you noticed it just now and it will keep on happening when your attention has moved elsewhere.

It's happening by itself, along with the digestion of your food and the circulation of your blood and the balancing of your hormones and the firing of neurons in your brain and literally countless other things.

So too, all of Existence is happening by itself. When we let go of all our judgments, we begin to cooperate with it, to dance with it. We begin to meet it just in the moment, without pre-conditions or stories. We begin to love it as it is.

Then we're turning on a light instead of fighting with darkness or the furniture. Then we're waking up from our waking dream of stories about Reality, and we find that our problems either disappear or that we can approach them in a more fruitful way.

Reversing the flow.

Gratitude also reverses the flow of clinging. Instead of complaining about whatever, we tune into the perfect imperfection of Existence, including ourselves, and we begin to take joy in it. We let go.

We begin to tune into the incredible beauty of it all, including the waves and violets and even all the "wrong" things we see.

All of it is necessary, ceaselessly weaving back and forth between day and night, winter and summer, sunshine and rain, health and disease, youth and old age, winning and losing, pleasure and pain, joy and sorrow, life and death, darkness and light.

CHAPTER 6

LOVE

The greatest achievement, in my opinion, is not to be some superhuman person who never feels the ordinary human feelings of grief or fear or pain. All of that is just as much a part of life as joy, excitement and pleasure.

Our impulses are almost constantly tugging at us. "Do this," they say. "Do that." Cajoling us through our desires and judgments and aversions and so on.

But we can just watch all that. That's what the Buddha and many other people pointed out. We can just watch those impulses and stories and let them be there.

We can let them appear on their own and disappear on their own without buying into them, without picking them up. We can accept that they're there without acting on them.

We can watch them, just like watching leaves floating down a stream, or clouds floating across the sky, or waves rising and falling. They rise and fall by themselves if we just watch them without identifying with them.

Silence helps a lot with this. "Silence is the greatest teacher," Ramana Maharshi said.

Just going into a period of sitting in silence every day, and watching the parade of desires and intentions and resentments and stories and beliefs surface again and again in our mind helps us to see that they're just productions and projections of the mind.

This quality of bare witnessing of our internal stream of thoughts and feelings, using the same love and acceptance that we can bring to the outside world, has been called vipassana, mindfulness, bare attention, and many other things.

Basically it means being aware of our thoughts and feelings as just thoughts and feelings. It means accepting them and watching them but giving them no energy, not getting involved. The alternative is to identify with the thoughts and go off on a "train of thought." That's our living, waking daydream of being fast asleep.

When we can just watch that whole internal parade, with great love and acceptance but without identifying with it, we have more equanimity about it all. We're more willing to let things flow into and out of our life, to love this life as it is.

We know that everything will change and that everything and everybody that appears in our life will disappear someday, that whatever is born will die, that whatever or whoever feels pleasure will also have to feel pain. And we can make our peace with all of that.

We can surrender, as Mohammed, Rumi, Hafez, Rabiya and other mystic and poetic Muslims and Sufis have recommended.

To what? To the Beloved, to Existence itself, from which we have never ever been separate. So in a sense we surrender to ourselves, to Life. We surrender to the great and majestic Mystery that we can't really understand.

Is this process done all at once? No more than a farmer can plant seeds and harvest all at once. It takes time and patience. And of course we'll have many "setbacks," times when we can't be as conscious or as loving as at other times. That's all part of the process too.

If we meet in the supermarket tomorrow, will you necessarily find me loving and kind and conscious? Not necessarily. Maybe I'm having a bad day. Maybe I didn't sleep last night. Maybe I'm caught up in some drama or story in that moment and I'm not as awake or kind to you as I would wish to be when I'm more relaxed.

Your journey is the same in that respect. There will be times when you're caught in some way, when you're identifying with the belief or story and you're contracted inside. It's all just part of it.

When we do contract inside, we can say "yes" to that too; we can say "yes to the no."

When we contract, and we will many times, we can love that contraction too, and just keep coming back to our intention to nurture our heart and the garden of this world as best we can.

We can just water that seed each day and it will sprout and blossom in its own time.

From one point of view we're just molecules and atoms and quarks ceaselessly vibrating and interweaving and sometimes spraying up as a "Mary" or a "Bill" or a "willow tree" or a "daisy" for a little while.

From another point of view, if we pull back to the viewpoint of the immensely vast stretch of galaxies, we're not even as noticeable as a grain of sand on the beach.

And here we are in between for a little while.

And during that little while, love is all that really matters. Isn't it true? When we're lying on our deathbed, as dying people report, we mainly remember the times others loved us and the times we loved them.

CHAPTER 7

LOVE II

Love is all that really matters.

Not just love for our loved ones, those who treat us well, but love for everything that's left over too, as Jesus said. Even love for our "enemies" in this drama. Yes to everything in this beautiful, mysterious Existence.

Love that's not conditional on something or someone being some way, that's not addressed to somewhere in particular, that doesn't leave any being or thing out.

Then our greatest achievement as humans is just to live an ordinary life. To love and laugh and cry and weep bitter tears at times, and wash the dishes and take care of each other.

To water the garden and prepare the meals and deal with the problems and raise our children as best we can and love the whole process of it all, knowing that we'll make many "mistakes."

Knowing that this little spray that the ocean has thrown up is perfectly imperfect in its ordinariness and humanness, and that that is its greatness.

To accept our humanity is to accept that we're all saint and sinner, we all have the potential of Hitler and Mother Teresa inside.

So we study the process we're going through on the way to some ideal, because we know that the process is the real product. We know that the means we use to achieve some great end is the real end we achieve.

Accepting our humanity means accepting that we're capable of being insensitive and cruel at one moment and kind and compassionate at another, intelligent and wise at one time and ignorant and foolish at another.

As humans we embody many contradictions, just as all beings do and as Existence itself does.

When we can accept and love those contradictions in ourselves and others and the world, and just keep patiently nurturing our love of Existence, pointing out what's beautiful and true in each person, how magnificent they are in their ordinary beingness, then the divine is coming through us and once again showing up on earth. In your heart. In my heart.

Then the Ocean is expressing its Heart through your wave or my wave. But really there is no "your wave" or "my wave." It's all just the Ocean doing it. It's the Ocean that's doing everything whatsoever.

And we can trust That, without feeling that it needs to look some particular way or to reach some particular outcome. We can trust it knowing that the black clouds are as necessary as the white clouds, knowing that sadness is as necessary as joy and has its own beauty.

We can trust the same Existence that's beating our heart to take care of everything else too, in a way that we can't really understand with our mind but we can feel with our heart.

So we do what we do. We play our part as impeccably and kindly as we can, knowing all the while that it's a great privilege to be here, to be able to appreciate this Existence, to allow the Existence to appreciate Itself, so to speak, through us.

We nurture as best we can that seed in our heart, accepting our ordinary, magnificent and contradictory humanity along the way.

We nurture as best we can this seed that we call the world, accepting the magnificence of its ordinariness. A flower. A leaf. A pair of eyes. A heart. Yes, even our own ceaseless judgments about what's "good" and "bad."

Then that seed of love begins to grow to its natural potential, to evolve to the flower that lies within it. But there's no hurry. Everything takes its own time, like a field of flowers growing.

And we can cooperate with the vast blossoming of Existence by appreciating the way it is now, by allowing ourselves to see the perfection of that seed as it is now, and nurturing it as best we can. We do our best to turn on a light instead of cursing the darkness. Then things can evolve to whatever's next.

Lao-Tzu, the founder of Taoism, said:

"Rejoice in the way things are."

I love that. Notice that he didn't say to grudgingly put up with the way things are. No; he said:

"*Rejoice* in the way things are."

Rejoice in this world just as it is.

Rejoice in others just the way they are.

Rejoice in yourself just the way you are.

Rejoice in your life just the way it is.

Then you feel the blessing, whenever you do, of an opening heart. You feel the growing joy of appreciating Existence in all the forms it presents. You feel more and more in love with this beautiful Existence, which comes alive within your heart and the hearts of others.

PART 2
Spirit

CHAPTER 8

GENEROSITY

Each of us has a unique path in life. No one else's answers can truly be our answers. Only the answer that comes from within ourselves can truly be ours.

The Buddha said that 2500 years ago, and added, "Be a lamp unto yourselves." Jesus said, "The kingdom of heaven is within you." They and other great teachers seem to be pointing to something inside us as holding the key to life's mystery and meaning.

To convey what is found there, various mystical traditions have used a metaphor about the shining of the sun. When it's a cloudy day we sometimes say that the sun isn't shining. Yet if we climb a mountain or take a plane above the clouds, we immediately see that the sun is there, it's shining, and has always been shining.

That metaphor, the mystics say, is approximately our situation. We have a kind of sun shining inside of us, a warm, bright, loving intelligence that is always shining, but yet is obscured by clouds.

Those clouds, they say, are formed by our thoughts and images and desires and emotions and aversions and so on. All of that together is our "cloudy sky."

They also point out that it's not necessary to do anything about the sun. Rather, that once the clouds are no longer obscuring the sky, that the natural luminosity of our essential nature reveals itself inherently.

If *Part 1–Heart,* is grounded in the teachings of Jesus, then this *Part 2–Spirit* is grounded in the teachings of the Buddha, though it also includes other teachers and personal experience.

The Buddha was very brilliant and compassionate, but also extremely practical—he was interested in showing us how to do things for ourselves. This Part 2, then, attempts to embody that how-to-do-it emphasis.

Those in all ages who have gone within invite us to do it too and find for ourselves our essential nature. And they promise that if we do, it will transform our life.

These words are about that inner journey.

It's a journey that I'm travelling also. In part these words are for my own sake, to increase my own clarity in taking this journey myself. And I'd love it if these words could somehow benefit you.

The Buddha suggested beginning the inner journey with the cultivation of the quality of *generosity,* and then what he called the *precepts.*

And he gave a very interesting reason for following these suggestions for outer behavior. Because following these "skillful means," as he called them, would tend to quiet down the stormiest or most cloudy waves of the mind and thus be very helpful to our journey inward.

He pointed out that if we're acting unethically, or "unskillfully" as he said, our journey within will be very difficult because the mind will be too agitated or numbed out. So these are measures taken in everyday life that allow the mind to find the beginnings of peace.

Generosity is cultivated as a kind of training wheels for the mind. It's a good antidote to the mind's usual tendency to cling—to objects, beliefs, desires, stories about other people, etc. This clinging tendency was identified by the Buddha as the root cause of suffering.

Generosity reverses the flow of our mind's clinging and grasping. When we look for ways to be generous, we immediately increase our own sense of well-being and happiness. Generosity tends to open up the mind's sense of tightness, allowing it to begin to relax.

So, to begin, we can practice giving to others. This can range from doing a favor to saying a kind word. A great sense of lightness comes over us when we begin to look for ways to be generous without thought of return.

It's a great paradox, too, but the more valuable the things that we give away—"Oh no, I couldn't give *that* away"—the lighter we feel.

Being generous to others also means adopting a non-harming attitude towards them, and here we'll talk about the precepts.

Later on, when the mind begins to open to its own luminosity, our actions will be a spontaneous and unique intuitively moral response to each situation. It will naturally tend towards the most harmonious outcome for all concerned. But for now we cultivate skillful actions to reduce impediments to the mind's inward journey.

The first precept is not to physically harm others, that is, not to kill them, strike them and so on. Such unskillful actions create great turmoil.

The second precept is not to steal from others—that is, not to take from somebody or an organization something that hasn't been offered, or hasn't been offered in the way that we're thinking of taking it.

The third precept is not to be unskillful in speaking with others. This includes following our inner truth in saying "yes" or "no," avoiding harsh and unkind speech to others, and avoiding untruthful speech, all of which feed the mind's tendency to tighten.

The fourth precept concerns the sexual and romantic area. Since this is such a strong drive, the tendency to manipulate others in this area is strong. We act skillfully in this area by avoiding manipulations of others and by respecting their right to whatever boundaries they deem appropriate.

The basic thrust of these precepts is to put into practice Jesus' Golden Rule—that is, to treat others as we would like them to treat us.

The fifth precept is to avoid intoxicants of various kinds, everything from nicotine to alcohol to uppers and downers and hallucinogens, anything that can cloud the mind and reduce its essential brightness. We could say that this is going for a different kind of "high," what we might call a Clarity High.

The initial purpose of these actions, again, is for our own sake—to reduce as much as possible actions that tend to greatly disturb or cloud the mind and thus reduce its capacity to undertake the inward journey.

CHAPTER 9

HINDRANCES

Next we become aware of what are known as the *hindrances*, that is, states of mind that disturb the mind's essential luminosity, both in everyday life and in sitting meditation.

We accept these hindrances to whatever extent that they're there, but we begin to pay attention. We begin to notice how they disturb the mind's essential stability and peace. Over time, in doing this, we develop a natural equanimity towards these states of mind; that is, we can watch them without feeling that we need to act on them. We begin to see the robotic nature of the hindrances.

The first is *greed*, which can come in various hues, whether for money or power or sensuality or the desire to be right. It's not that we reject greed or any of the other hindrances—they'll come up whenever they do—but we begin to watch them rather than act them out.

This hindrance of greed can be compared to water in which a red dye has been placed. Even a relatively small amount of dye can render opaque a large amount of water and prevent the observer from seeing to the stillness of the bottom.

The second hindrance is the opposite of the first, that is, *aversion* of various kinds. This includes when our mind goes to places of ill-will, anger, hatred, irritation, discontent and so on. Again, we don't try to repress these feelings, but we do bring attention to them; we begin to notice how they deeply unsettle the mind. In that very noticing, they begin to gradually become more flimsy.

This hindrance has been compared to water that is boiling, and thus opaque in that way to seeing down into the depths of the water.

The third hindrance is *laziness and dullness.* Here we notice the mind's tendency sometimes to fall into a state of numbness, where it doesn't want to notice the reality of what is going on inside. The mind distracts itself in various ways—anything from zealotry to drugs to shopping to TV to compelling ideas will do—and thus dulls itself in a kind of sleepiness, so that it cannot perceive its inherent warm and loving brightness. So we begin to notice the times when we've dulled ourselves in some way.

This hindrance has been compared to water overgrown by weeds and algae, so that once again the depths of the water cannot be seen.

The fourth hindrance is the opposite of the third, that is, *restlessness* in its different forms, which includes worry and agitation and fear. Again, it's not that we try to repress restlessness or fear when it appears, but we do begin to notice the mind's tendency to go there when it imagines that things or situations or people have to be a certain way that *it* thinks is best.

When we judge that someone should be different then we're in their business instead of our own—and we begin to notice how we suffer when we get into someone else's business.

This hindrance has been compared to water that is swept by fierce winds, so that the water is no longer transparent and naturally clear.

The fifth hindrance is *skeptical doubt,* which can prevent us from undertaking any worthwhile path of growth. This usually takes two forms: One is nihilism—"This world is illusory and empty and nothing matters, so there's no point in exerting myself."

The other pole of doubt is eternalism—"All these glittering objects in the world are real and exist independently and are the source of happiness, so I'll just devote myself to grasping and indulging in them. What's the point of looking into my inner world?"

This hindrance has been compared to water that is in darkness, so that once again the depths of it cannot be observed and experienced.

These hindrances were set out by the Buddha many years ago, but they are equally relevant now because awareness of them is still very conducive to seeing how the mind disturbs its essential peace.

When the hindrances arise, we let them settle down by letting them be there and shifting to watching them instead of grabbing them and acting on them. It's kind of like sitting on the bank of a muddy pond and watching the mud settle by itself.

CHAPTER 10

UNDOING

The third facet of this inward journey, in my opinion, is the work of the teacher Byron Katie.

It might seem strange that right in the middle of the Buddha's insights I start talking about Byron Katie. But I'd be remiss if I didn't. Of all the many approaches to personal development that I've looked into, Katie's seems to me the simplest and yet the most profound. To me it seems an indispensable tool in helping to undo the mind and thus to facilitate the journey within.

My description of Katie's work is just my personal understanding, so you may want to contact her center directly to hear a tape or attend a gathering. In addition, Katie has sheets and booklets to assist with the process of The Work, and they can also be obtained by contacting

The Work Foundation at www.thework.org or at (760) 256-5653 in Barstow, CA.

The Work begins by writing down something that bothers or upsets us. We write it down to stop the mind, to photograph it for a moment so that we can better work with it. In doing this we allow that petty, judgmental part of us to fully express. As Katie says, we've been instructed for years not to judge, and it's still what we do best.

Thus we drop for a moment any spiritual insights that we may have picked up, and let ourselves really feel and express the hurt child inside.

Experienced students of the Work sometimes just write down their stream-of-thought about something that's bothering them, and begin the Inquiry right from there. Katie provides sheets to assist in writing down our complaints in a more structured form, asking ourselves questions such as:

Concerning this person or situation, what is it that's bothering me? How should they or it be different? What do I want them to do? What are my opinions of them? What is it I don't ever want to experience again?

In writing these things, we deliberately project our attention outside—that is, we judge our neighbor or some situation rather than ourselves. The reason for this will become evident a little later.

Once we have our upset feelings written down in a series of statements, we then begin to investigate those statements. Basically, we inquire about their truthfulness and their effects upon us.

So we ask ourselves inside, "Is this belief true? Can I really know that it's true?" When we go within and really look at the belief we discover that we can't be certain of it and that no belief or story is really true. Every belief is just a story of some kind that we've got going and that we've velcroed to.

Then we ask ourselves the question, "What do I get from holding this belief?" And variations of it, such as: How do I live when I hold this belief? How do I treat myself and others when I hold it? Can I see a reason to hold onto it other than suffering?

When we really look inside we find that holding on to the belief is causing us misery and suffering and feelings of isolation and separation. We see that clearly, we feel it acutely.

Then we look at the other side, the positive side: "Who would I be without this belief?" How would I act, how would I live? When we really look, we usually find that without the belief we would be much more free and available, much more open and joyful.

It can have a powerful effect to look at the truth of our stories and then examine the costs of holding on to them and the benefits of letting go.

But then Katie gives us the kicker; she has us reverse everything. Every statement that we've written down, we turn it around. If we've written down, "Ellen is insensitive towards me," we turn it around to, "I am insensitive towards Ellen."

And then we really look inside to see if we can find the turn-around. We look to see if the reversal statement isn't at least as true as the original one.

And it's the most amazing thing—when we truly look, we find that we've been doing to the other person what we've accused them of doing to us. Sometimes we've been doing it overtly, and sometimes just in our mind.

Let's take an example: A friend called the other day and said that her fiance was "too much in his head" and "hasn't made love to me in weeks."

The first statement, turned around, became "I am too much in my head." She had the courage to look at that, and found it: She *was* too much in her head lately, especially when she was judging her fiance to be too much in his head.

Then she turned around the second statement and it became, "I haven't made love to him in weeks." This puzzled her; she couldn't find it. Then I asked her if she had made love to her fiance in her mind lately, that is, had she been kind to him in her mind?

And then she found it. Yes, she had been very unkind toward him lately in her mind, criticizing and judging him a lot. So, really, she had not been making love to him lately. The turn-around was true.

Then she turned it around again. "I have not been making love to myself lately." She saw how true that was, how harsh she'd been with herself lately, and she cried.

When she saw this and some other things she lightened up tremendously, and suddenly felt a great sense of compassion towards her fiance—and herself. That is the power of Katie's work.

The purpose of these questions and turn-arounds isn't to whitewash anything, but to clearly see that the universe comes in dualities, and that what we accuse others of doing we're doing ourselves as well. If I think someone is being arrogant, *I'm* being arrogant in the moment of judging them as arrogant. To see this is very freeing.

Fundamentally, other people don't cause us to feel anything. If we didn't have a particular quality ourselves, we would have no emotional charge upon that quality in someone else. We might notice it, we might even think it fascinating, but we would not be disturbed by it.

For instance, let's suppose we're upset that "Joe is such an angry person." We see that it's *our* unconscious pool of anger—probably picked up in childhood and repressed—that is being denied and projected out.

In this example, Joe is doing or saying whatever he does or says. It's our mind that judges that wrong, or says that it shouldn't be that way, as if we know God's business better than God, as if the universe ought to conduct itself according to *our* ideas of how it should be.

In this example, if we didn't have that deep pool of unconscious anger in ourselves, we wouldn't have any particular charge on Joe's anger. We wouldn't have any energy on it; it would just be a fact.

The clue that something within ourselves is being stimulated by Joe is that we have an emotional charge about it. Then we know that it's not Reality but our disagreement with Reality that's causing us to suffer.

Reality is just the way it is. When we're in disagreement with Reality, we suffer. And it's our own disavowed quality inside that is causing us to suffer, in this case the anger we feel that's being generated internally but, we say, "caused" by Joe.

We look and see the truth—that we're causing our experience of Reality ourselves. Our internal experience is being self-generated based on past traumas and conditionings. It's stimulated by external events but not caused by them.

Here we're looking at the truth of our projections upon the world and other people. And because the world is just a big mirror to us, we understand who it is that we're really seeing and describing in our story. The only person we ever really see or describe is ourselves. What we see in others exists in us.

Then, the very thing that we said we weren't willing to experience again, we say that we *are willing* to experience it again. We say that and open to it. "I'm willing to experience this again," because it almost certainly will happen again—only this time we want to respond to it in a more open and transparent way.

And then we say and feel, "I *look forward* to experiencing this again." That final statement releases our grip on the story even more.

In my experience, Katie's work opens us up like nothing else. There are many, many valuable body-mind approaches out there, and I honor them all and have received benefit from many of them. I emphasize Katie's work because it's brilliant and deep and has great compassion as well. In my opinion, we're fortunate to have her on the planet.

CHAPTER 11

BREATH

Another aspect of the inward journey is to begin to deliberately cultivate profound states of concentration of the body-mind, both for their relaxing effect and also to prepare the mind for insight meditation.

This is done by refining concentration into a meditation, also known as tranquillity meditation.

Concentration is something that we all partake of to some extent. When we're focused on writing a term paper, making love or accomplishing a goal at work, we're partaking of the rudimentary stages of concentration meditation. But now we deliberately focus and intensify this effect.

In concentration meditation we focus the mind upon a single point of attention and return it there again and again. The mind doesn't want to do this at first, because it is accustomed to roaming around at will. Our normal mind is sometimes compared to a drunken monkey swinging chaotically through the trees. Now we're going to focus.

Often, when beginning concentration meditation, the mind will seem even more restless than usual. It's not, but in attempting to focus the mind on one point we'll begin to see just how restless our mind really is. Because it will go away to other things again and again. And each time we notice that, we can just gently return attention back to the concentration object.

One of the benefits of concentration is that by and by the mind will actually come into the present moment, as the organism slows down. More and more, the mind will be able to put down temporarily its burden of thoughts and judgments and cravings and conditionings—and the suffering they bring.

In concentration meditation, the mind's thoughts and conditionings are temporarily swept aside so that the mind can experience its innate spaciousness and brightness. When we stop doing the meditation, though, we come down from this "high."

But while its effects are temporary, concentration nevertheless is highly valuable both for giving a taste of what true liberation would actually be like, and also as a powerful tool for the next stage.

Our concentration object can be any number of things. It can be a *mantra,* for instance—a word or phrase such as "Rama" or "Allah" or "O Gracious God, have mercy on me," or "May all beings be happy" or "Om Mane Padme Hum" (the jewel in the lotus). I've tried all of these and others and have found all of them to be effective.

Another possibility is a visual image of some kind. A *mandala* is such a visual image, usually of circles within circles. A *kasina* is a colored disc about the size of a dinner plate that one focuses on. Other examples could be a candle flame, a flower, the picture of one's guru or of someone who especially inspires us. The latter will arouse devotion, adding to the concentration.

One can also concentrate on a kinesthetic motion, such as Sufi whirling or rocking one's arm or body back and forth.

But having tried these and others, I have to admit to a bias in the end, because in my experience nothing compares with using the breath as one's object of concentration.

It's not an accident that the mystical tradition of virtually every spiritual path has some emphasis upon the breath—because the breath is so fundamental to us, it's so natural to our life as human beings.

The breath has many great qualities as a concentration object. First, it is always available under all circumstances. We are breathing from the moment we are born to the moment we die.

Second, it does not give rise to any hindrances, or emotional imbalances. Concentration upon things such as piling up money or power can lead to disturbances of the mind. Some phrases—examples might be "I am all-powerful" or "Death cannot touch me"—could also give rise to disturbances in the mind.

A third advantage of the breath is that it has no concepts associated with it. It's a purely natural process, part of nature, associated with the present moment rather than any concepts. The Buddha, who was among other things a consummate concentration master, chose the breath as his own object of concentration.

A final advantage to using the breath is that, unlike some other objects, it can lead to the highest states of concentration—what are known as the *jhanas,* or states of profound absorption.

We begin, normally, by sitting down. We can also lie down, but the risk of that position is sleepiness. We want to stay quite awake, so normally we sit up.

Sitting can be done on a cushion or in a chair.

On a cushion sitting can be done in the classic lotus or half-lotus posture, or in other positions where the legs are folded more casually. Or we can sit in a chair. The more we sit up straight in the chair, the more awake we'll tend to be.

The idea is just that we want to get into a position where we can remain stable and awake for a period of time. If we have to shift positions frequently, our meditation will suffer. The calmer and more stable our body is, the calmer and more stable the mind will be.

For the purposes of sitting meditation, a place that is quiet and undisturbed is ideal. We want to remove, as far as possible, all sources of distraction, so we can concentrate all our attention on the meditation object.

It's good to determine the length of the meditation before we go into it. If we leave it up to our whims, we tend to have short sessions because the mind will supply reasons to end the session prematurely. A timer is helpful since it's distracting to keep glancing at a watch.

To begin with, 20 or 30 minutes is good. Even 10 minutes will be beneficial. Over several months we can work up to sessions of an hour. A nice rhythm is to do half an hour in the morning and half an hour after work or before sleep. Experienced meditators often work three or four hours of meditation into their daily activities.

Normally we close our eyes. But we can do it with eyes open too. In that case we simply let our eyes gaze on a floor or wall a few feet in front of us, but without focusing on anything in particular.

Now we just watch the breath with our attention as it flows in and out. We watch the breath flow into our bodies and we watch it flow out without trying to control it in any way. This is not about breath control, but about watching without interference.

As we just watch our breath, it will naturally slow down and become calmer and more stable. This process calms the sympathetic nervous system (fight or flight system) and promotes the parasympathetic nervous system instead (the relaxing and calming system).

To increase our concentration further, we want to sharpen our focus. We do this by fixing our attention upon the breath at a specific area.

One possibility is to use the rising and falling of the belly (*hara* in Zen) for this purpose. As the breath goes in, the belly rises; as it goes out, the belly falls. We can observe this rising and falling with our attention.

That is a good choice, and I worked with it for a long time. We often hold much of our unconscious tension in our bellies, and one of the advantages of focusing in this area is the reduction of that tension. Watching the breath at the belly is profoundly relaxing and can serve as a good anchor when we begin insight meditation, discussed a bit later.

But the object I have come to favor is the one most likely used by the Buddha himself, that is, watching the breath where it first comes into the body, at the nose.

When we take a breath, the air first strikes our nostrils at a certain point. For most people this point is at the inside tip of the nose, though for some it will be near the upper lip. We can experiment for ourselves: Take a few deep breaths through your nose and see where the initial sensation of the breath is most prominent.

This point where the breath is first noticed is called the *phusana,* the contact point. We now focus our attention there, watching the breath at that point.

In doing so, we emulate a gatekeeper. A gatekeeper lets people in or out, but doesn't follow them once they've passed the gate. In similar fashion, we watch the breath at the nose but no longer follow it into the body. We want to sharply focus our attention, and for that purpose the breath at the tip of the nose is ideal.

An amazing thing happens when we watch our breath in this way. Over time the breath becomes alive. It always was, of course, but we didn't notice it before. Now we're studying it, not by thinking about it, but directly, just watching it intently.

The breath has much to teach us about the cycles of life. We cannot have only in-breaths or only out-breaths, but must have both. As we watch the breath, it teaches us much about the dual nature of Existence, how the leaves and roots of the tree always exist together, how pleasure and pain, winning and losing must both be there.

But beyond that, the breath at this sharply focused point becomes a doorway into another dimension, the dimension of the present moment, the dimension where all true spiritual journeys begin.

As we meditate in this way, our attention will be distracted countless times onto other things. We become distracted by a thought and follow it and it turns into another and another. Seconds or minutes later we notice that and, using mindful awareness, return our attention to the breath.

As we continue in this way, our meditation slowly deepens. We get distracted less often, and for shorter times. Our breath becomes more vivid, more present and alive. We begin to feel a sense of merging with it.

CHAPTER 12

LIGHT

As our concentration practice deepens, the mind settles down and begins to take a quiet joy in itself. We begin to experience the mind's essential nature as being bliss when it isn't burdened down by incessant thinking and painful feelings, by craving and aversion.

When the mind is well concentrated these things are temporarily suppressed from consciousness and so the mind gets a glimpse of its true, spacious nature.

But concentration meditation does not extinguish these things. Our stories and cravings and resentments and so on simply go to the unconscious and bide their time. Then, when our concentration meditation is over, they slowly return to consciousness. The taste of our true nature is temporary.

Nevertheless, this daily concentration on our breath accomplishes a great deal. The body-mind begins to relax on a deep level that's not really reached by anything else. You'll find that you're less reactive in your daily life, that you have more of a sense of humor, that you're more easy-going. You'll find that your interactions with people tend to be more harmonious, and that you tend to enjoy life more. You'll notice these things and more.

These tendencies are especially so if to some extent we continue to focus on our breath as we go about our daily life. Not a big deal, but just a sort of background awareness of our breath at the contact point as we listen and cook and work and so on. From time to time we'll recollect ourselves, and let some of our attention return to our breath as we go about our business.

As we quiet down a little inside, our intuition becomes greater. Not only do we find that we can trust life more and more, but that our intuitive sense of how to function effectively in various situations increases.

There's an inner knowing inside each of us, a warm, bright, loving intelligence—beneath the level of thoughts and beliefs and cravings—that has a great sense of how to act and what to do in our lives.

As meditation deepens, we find ourselves hearing this "inner guidance" more and listening to it and acting upon it more. And listening less to the craziness of our ordinary mind.

Any serious meditator sooner or later comes face to face with an astonishing realization: That his or her mind is completely crazy—that it's a chaotic, out-of-control bus careening madly down a steep hill with no brakes. It's always been that way, but we hadn't noticed it before because we were so caught up in it. Now we do notice, and it's a sobering moment when we really see it.

As meditators, as we become more relaxed we also become more tuned in to this inner guidance in our daily life. Whereas the thoughts of our ordinary mind tend to come from a need to feel safe, the intuitive wisdom of our inner guide comes from a different place.

Our inner guidance comes from a place of great love and possibility. As we quiet down a bit inside, this inner knowing, this warm bright intelligence within us begins to direct our activities more, and we find that we're spontaneously doing things without knowing why sometimes. But we're following our own inner truth more.

Not that it's always a picnic. Oftentimes my inner guide or intelligence has suggested something to which my rational mind reacts, "Whoa! That's crazy! I can't do that!" But increasingly I've just gone ahead and followed it anyway, and almost always things have turned out in fulfilling ways that I couldn't have imagined from my rational mind.

Another way of saying this is that as our trust in life increases, we open up more to whatever wants to happen.

We become more available to the Mystery of life and so more of that Mystery reveals Itself in our life.

It can seem pretty silly at times, I know, to sit there and watch our breath. The mind may remark what a silly thing it is, especially when we could be playing or doing something "productive." This kind of thought, that we're wasting our time, it isn't working and so on, will come up sooner or later when we're meditating.

We don't fight with these thoughts or doubts or judgments when they come up—that would be buying in and thus compounding the distraction—but just gently return the attention to the breath, over and over.

A time comes when our attention on the breath at the contact point becomes so alluring that our awareness of it becomes unbroken for periods of time.

Now, instead of having to exert energy to remain concentrated, the process seems to go on by itself. Our attention remains, for periods of time lasting from seconds to minutes, absorbed in the living sensation of the breath at a single point.

This is sometimes called "fixing" or the *preliminary sign.* It is a sign of increased concentration. This degree of concentration is sufficient to begin the practice of *insight* or *mindfulness meditation,* discussed in the next chapter. But it is possible to go further into concentration, and if we do, our insight meditation will greatly benefit because of the mind's greater deepening and ability to focus.

To go deeper into tranquillity, should we choose to do that, requires spending longer periods of time focused on our meditation. We may want to go on a meditation retreat at some point, whether privately or in a group, because it greatly increases our momentum.

When our awareness at the contact point is deep and unbroken enough for long enough, a new kind of sign will arise in our concentration. We will begin to see a light inside. This is the *nimitta* (the sign).

At first this light will be just a point of light, and it will be noticed where we've been concentrating our attention—at the tip of our nose. This point of light is called sometimes the *acquired sign,* because now we've acquired something new. We continue to watch our breathing, but gradually shift attention to the point of light itself.

As we do that, the point of light gradually becomes more vivid. It can begin to look like the sun or the moon or a wisp of smoke. It can begin to spread like stars in the evening, or become a brightness that paints the inner sky.

It can also move to a different location, either inside the body in the chest or belly, or out in "front" of one's closed eyes. It is different for each person.

When we've stabilized this sign, so we can acquire it whenever we like and maintain it for as long as desired, we're said to be in *neighborhood concentration.* It's called "neighborhood" because now we've in the neighborhood of the 1st Absorption.

It can be compared to the place, when driving into a city, where we pass the city limits. We're not downtown yet, but we've passed into the city.

We now direct our attention only to this stabilized inner light and hold our concentration there. As we do that, qualities of this unusual state begin to be noticed—sustained attention, extreme rapture, and bliss.

What we do now is subtly shift our attention to the qualities themselves. Our awareness of the breath and of the light remains, but they're no longer the focus. Instead we focus on these qualities of sustained attention, rapture and bliss; we "gather them in" until they are very strong and very steady. We're now in the 1st Absorption.

For the practice of mindfulness meditation, this degree of concentration is more than sufficient. In fact, we can begin mindfulness meditation with no preparation in concentration at all, in what's known as starting with "bare attention."

Or we can develop concentration to the level of the preliminary sign (an unbroken awareness of the breath), neighborhood concentration (the stabilized inner light), or the 1stAbsorption.

Though none of these is necessary, each increase in our concentration ability will help our mindfulness to go deeper and progress more easily.

It's also possible to go higher into the Absorptions if desired. In brief, to enter into each higher Absorption we let go of the crudest quality of the one below it. Thus to reach the 2nd from the 1st, we let go of awareness of sustained attention and focus on just rapture and bliss.

To reach the 3rd Absorption from the 2nd, we see that rapture is a gross quality compared to bliss; and so we let rapture go and focus on bliss and equanimity alone. To reach the 4th we see that bliss still has some disturbance compared to equanimity, and so we focus on the latter. And there are even higher ones.

All the Absorptions are extremely profound levels of tranquillity and peace. Why then would we want to go anywhere else? Isn't that the end of the journey?

CHAPTER 13

INSIGHT

That was the question the Buddha asked himself. He had studied under the foremost meditation masters of his day and had attained all eight levels of profound absorption. Yet he was brilliant and perceptive enough to realize that he still wasn't truly free, was not truly liberated from suffering yet.

How did he realize that? He noticed that no matter how "high" he got in the absorption levels, that he still came down from them. He noticed that when he stopped doing his profound concentrations, his normal crazy mind came back, complete with all its conditionings.

He noticed that while the five hindrances were completely absent while he was in the absorption levels, they were still there when he came down from his profound concentration. He was still capable of feeling ill-will or anxiety, of feeling restless or bored, of clutching at things in the world.

He noticed that he was still capable of suffering. He wasn't truly free of the problem of human suffering yet, and so true liberation was not yet his experience.

So he decided to try an experiment—he would go the other way. Instead of concentrating on one object, he would open his consciousness up to whatever wanted to be in his mind at the moment. But he decided to *observe* the motions of his mind rather than participating in them. And here was born the discovery of mindfulness meditation, surely one of the most momentous events in the whole history of humankind.

Mindfulness is something that we all have to some extent. Anytime we notice that something we've done has caused us suffering, anytime we notice that we're not getting the results we want, anytime we notice the rapidity with which one mind-state can change to another, we're using mindfulness.

When we're doing concentration meditation and we notice that our attention is distracted, it's mindfulness that does the noticing and then brings our attention back to the primary object.

So we all have some mindfulness. But now we want to deliberately cultivate it, like cultivating a garden, so that it becomes very powerful and steady.

What the Buddha did was to begin systematically studying his mind. Not by thinking about it, but just watching it in silence. Just watching it move.

In effect, the openness of the heart towards others and the world that Jesus preached about is now brought inside and applied to our own internal thought stream.

We take a step back from our thoughts and beliefs, desires and aversions, etc., and instead watch this inner thought stream with great love and acceptance. We become students of our own mind, to appreciate it and see how it works. Not by analyzing the mind or thinking about it, but by directly observing it.

What we normally do is this: We have some story or belief about somebody or something. And around that story or belief other stories and beliefs attach themselves. Now we have what's known as a "chain of thought."

This chain of thought is accompanied by an emotion, whether subtle or intense, and often a negative one. "They shouldn't have done that," goes the story, or "This world is rotten" or "John can't be trusted," or whatever. The number of possible complaints that our minds can generate is infinite.

Then what we normally do is take that chain of thought seriously and identify with it. It's not a belief, it's the "truth." We buy into the story or belief, we pick it up, we get involved with it. We think it's real, and then we act from that limited and conditioned place.

We spend most of our time believing in the truth and reality of our stories and beliefs. We look at life through the lenses of our stories and we take what we see there to be "the truth." But it's not. It's just a collection of stories that we tell about our experience of life.

In fact, as Byron Katie's work demonstrates so well, virtually any statement that we make about the world or other people can be turned around and applied to ourselves equally well or better.

If we have a belief that "Ellen is selfish when she ignores my wishes," we can turn that around to "I am selfish when I ignore Ellen's wishes," and we'll almost always find that the latter belief is at least as true as the former if we look honestly.

So what we see in the other is what we ourselves are doing, although perhaps in a different form. If we say "The world is awful," we can turn it around, substitute "my thinking" for "the world," and say "My thinking is awful." If we really look, we'll find it.

When we actually begin to see this, we understand that no belief or story is true; they're just stories in the mind that affect our experience of reality and stimulate us to feel pleasure or pain.

In Katie's work, we write the mind down on paper so that we can stop it and look at it, inquire about it. When we begin mindfulness meditation, we're doing the same thing in effect, but now we're doing it in real-time.

We're watching our thoughts and feelings and clingings moment-to-moment as they arise.

In effect, we do a new type of concentration meditation, where the object of concentration is continually changing—the object being the stream of thoughts and feelings in our own mind.

Here's where our development of concentration is so useful, because now we make use of that concentration to observe the moment-to-moment fluctuations of the mind itself. And the more developed our concentration, the more penetrating will be this observation of the mind's content at each moment.

Instead of "thinking our thoughts," going off on a chain of thought and taking our story seriously, we step back from it. We observe it with compassion and love, allowing it to be what it is, no longer trying to change it or improve it or deny it, but to just watch it.

And when we do that we see that each thought that arises, each desire or aversion or fear that arises has its own life cycle. It arises by itself, it stays in consciousness for a moment, and then falls away—to be immediately replaced by the next one.

We see that our thoughts and feelings and desires come on their own and go on their own if we don't get involved with them. They come and go like clouds in the sky come and go, like leaves floating down a stream come and go, if we don't interfere by giving them energy.

In concentration we were like a gatekeeper, staying aware of the breath at that one point but not following it in or out. Now, in insight meditation we do something similar—we observe the fluctuations of our mind from one moment to the next without following any of them anywhere, without going downstream with them.

We stop getting involved. We observe the mind moving around in its kaleidoscope of mind-states without clinging to it as much as before. It sounds unusual at first, but we develop compassion for our own mind as we come to see its desperation and craziness, as we begin to really see its fear and clutching.

In doing this, it helps very much to have an anchor, something we can hold onto for some stability and balance while we're investigating the thought stream of our mind. This is where our concentration meditation comes in again, because we use the same awareness of the breath at one point that we used before, only this time as an anchor for watching the mind's thought stream.

The mind jumps around so much and is so compelling in its stories that it would be easy to stay lost in them without an anchor. Watching our breath at the contact point turns out to be an ideal anchor. That sensation is there all the time, always available in the present, yet involves no concepts itself.

So when we go off on a chain of thought or get distracted by something—and we notice that we've done that—we once more return our attention to the breath at the contact point. But now we add something else.

Using the breath as our anchor, we now *invite* all the distractions and hindrances and conditionings. We invite all the thoughts and feelings and attachments because we want to watch them.

Instead of holding the mind solely to one point, we do hold that point but then also welcome the mind to behave normally.

And we watch it.

CHAPTER 14

MYSTERY

Now we watch the proceedings of the mind, using our anchor as a base. We let the mind do exactly what it wants to do, because we want to observe what it normally does, how it normally behaves.

And in the very process of observing calmly without interfering, various conditionings and stories rise up out of the unconscious and take center stage at various times. We see the whole parade and just watch it without adding energy to it.

As we do so, those conditionings in our mind gradually get less vivid, less forceful. As we watch, our whole thinking-feeling-desiring-rejecting mechanism begins to gradually slow down and become less solid.

By the power of our mindfulness, our conditioning,

ous ways of acting out, our mind's tendency to clutch at and grab and cling and reject becomes more transparent; we see how it is. We begin to truly know ourselves.

We see that everything in Existence is in ceaseless flux, constantly changing, so that we'll always be involved in either grasping towards something we don't have or clinging to something that can't stay the same. To clearly see the mind's innate tendency to do this is to understand the basic suffering of human life.

We clearly see that impersonal energies and forces are intermingling and producing everything, and that we ourselves are the result of such impersonal interactions of energies. That is, there is no real separate self.

As we watch our mind carefully, the whole notion of "I" as something existing separately begins to weaken. We see that our sense of "I" is composed of all the thoughts that we have about ourselves—that we literally create this illusion called "I" by weaving a web of almost ceaseless thoughts about it.

In other words, we think about ourselves a lot and so create this sense of existing separately from the rest of creation. And because we have this thought-nest of ideas and feelings about ourselves, continuously being renewed in our thought stream, we sense strongly that we exist as a separate "I."

But it's all an illusion, a sleight of hand. There's nobody home. What we experience as "I" is just thoughts and feelings in our mind, like flickering images on a movie screen creating the illusion of solidity. Flickering thoughts and feelings and desires of our mind create the illusion of solid "I," of something existing separately.

Naturally then, since we feel separate, we feel we have to manipulate the world in order to get what we want. And we feel suffering in doing so. Deep down, the mind feels isolated and lonely.

But as we use our mindfulness to see more clearly the impermanence, unsatisfactoriness and absence-of-self in life, a strange thing happens. We also come more and more into contact with the warm, luminous, loving intelligence at the core of us, that *is* us.

This natural essence inside is empty of all concepts and qualities, so when our minds are busy with thoughts we tend to think that it's not there. But it's always there, shining as our natural Mind. The cloud-thoughts of our thinking/desiring mind can obscure but never eliminate its luminous existence, constantly shining.

Our mindfulness gradually uncovers *that,* our true nature. But not just in meditation. Our times of sitting in meditation are really just training wheels again. We practice mindfulness in silence and solitude so that we can take it out into the world in our daily activities.

In effect, the times of sitting meditation recharge our mindfulness so that we can more powerfully use it the rest of the time, in our everyday life.

Over time we develop the ability to be mindful while we're reading or shaving or conversing or working, and as we do so our mindfulness gradually begins to become more and more unbroken. After a long while it begins to go on more or less continuously, whether eating or sleeping or meditating.

People who want to go all the way to Liberation tend to retreat to solitary places, forests and monasteries and so on where they can build up their mindfulness undisturbed by interruptions, a mindfulness that can continue unbroken more and more.

As that happens the mind becomes peaceful and quiet inside. Its conditionings and stories slowly fade out of view until time itself ceases to exist and there is only the present moment, timeless and eternal. Now we see Reality without filters, because we are no longer caught in our cravings and rejections and stories about it.

Now there is only the luminous warmth and love of innate Mind, with no separate "I" there to obscure it anymore. The illusion of the separate controller/doer is gone, and now Existence itself acts through us. We move then by "intuition," by an inner and vast Intelligence moving through us and as us.

And a moment comes when it becomes clear that the mindfulness is continuous and spacious and eternal and that it will always be this way and has always been this way and is this way now in the eternal moment.

In effect, time is gone, because there are no comparisons going on. Fear is gone because "Yes!" is said to everything. The state of mind is choicelessness, though Energy does move through the vessel. Feeling separate is gone because there is no one around to experience it.

This is sometimes called the "Moment of Maturity" or the moment of Liberation, what the Buddha called Nirvana. It's the moment when one ceases to exist—and yet continues to exist as a mind-body organism. But now this organism is transparent, available, and Intelligence moves through it, like the ocean rising in a wave.

Then this person does whatever they do. The great mystic Jacob Boehm was a cobbler by trade and remained one. Nisargadatta was a tobacco seller in Bombay and remained one. The master Ikkyu continued to be a homeless wanderer, as did also the Sufi Shams-e-Tabriz. Many began to teach. Because they're no longer acting out the conditioned mind, their actions are not predictable.

One who has become Self-realized now lives in the world but not of it, as Jesus said. They create a widening ripple of love and clarity, just from their being, just from whatever interactions they have with others.

They may or may not be found feeding the poor or bathing lepers. Francis of Assisi did that. But it's impossible to say what they'll do, because there's no set model any more. They simply respond to each situation from their innate Intelligence, not knowing how or why, just doing it and noticing that their actions tend to produce greater harmony for all concerned.

Jesus was there. The great Zen masters Sosan and Dogen and Hakuin were there. So were the great Tibetan masters Padmasambhava, Milarepa and Princess Tsogyal. So were Teresa of Avila, Juan de la Cruz and Meister Eckhardt. So too the Baal Shem Tov. The great mystics Mohammed and Rabia and Hafez. Lao-Tzu. Ramana Maharshi and Osho. Byron Katie and Ammachi and many, many others from all traditions.

They awoke to their fundamental nature and that awakening transformed their little life into an expression of Life, of God showing up on earth. We humans have benefitted incomparably from those among us who have woken up to their true nature.

But we need not wait until liberation to benefit. The image of a meditator is sometimes that of a monk removed from the world, oblivious to its concerns, but meditation in everyday life contributes greatly to our own life and the world around us.

As mindfulness permeates our life more, our conditionings and clingings slowly decrease, our mind-waves gradually slow down, our actions and speech naturally express more love and generosity. Our life tends toward a natural integrity then, not from following a set of rules, but from our increasing recognition of who we are and who others are.

This beneficial tendency can become especially pronounced when we consciously take our meditation into everyday activities. We use our sitting meditation each day to recharge our mindfulness, so that it can be more readily used in the rest of our life.

As we do that, we find ourselves more possessed of a certain stability, a certain feeling of well-being which is not so dependent on circumstance, a feeling of greater relaxation and tranquillity in the midst of the roller-coaster of life.

We also notice that the natural warm Intelligence inside begins to be more present, and to act through us. We become more detached about the ups and downs of life—and yet, paradoxically, more alive to life too, more present and available to its richness and beauty.

We find that things tend to "happen by themselves" more, with less pushing on our part. We find that we're more willing to let things and people be as they are, and that we want to love and nurture them more. And in the light of that love, we all mature more. The world loves itself more. God shows up again on earth—in us.

As that happens, then Love begins to fall in love with Itself again. We become happy just to be who we are, where we are, how we are, feeling what we're feeling. We naturally become more loving towards the universe because we increasingly know that we're not ever separate from it.

We expand, we open, we become more available to Life, to Existence however it wants to present itself. We become more available to this great Mystery that pervades us and flows through us, and through the atoms and the stars and the grass growing in the night.

To beautiful you—

May you experience much kindness and serenity until we meet again.

Love,

Jimmy Sloman

Jimmy Sloman is an investigative writer whose subject is the human condition. He has sought understanding from a wide range of great teachers past and present, famous and obscure, and traditions ranging from India to the kitchen table.

Thank you for reading *May You Be Happy.*

Products by Jimmy Sloman, and available through OceanBlue Publishing, include:

May You Be Happy, non-fiction
Handbook for Humans, non-fiction
Nothing, non-fiction
The Ripple, fiction
Songs From The Bottom Of The Sea, music album
Affecting Our Reality, recorded talk

Descriptions begin on the following page.

To order OceanBlue products by mail, please use the order form in the back.

To order products by phone, please call:

(800) 852-4890 (U.S., 24 hours)

(707) 838-6200 (abroad, 9-5 PST)

OceanBlue Publishing
98 Main St, Tiburon, CA 94920
www.ocean-blue.com (site available Feb '99)

May You Be Happy

14 chapters, $11.95

May You Be Happy is divided into two parts, *Heart* and *Spirit.*

Part 1, *Heart,* the first seven chapters, is grounded in the teachings of Jesus, though many other teachers are included. It is about opening the heart and beginning to fall in love with the world.

Part 2, *Spirit,* chapters 8 through 14, is grounded in the teachings of the Buddha, though again other teachers are included. This part, reflecting the practical, how-to-do-it emphasis of the Buddha, talks about the inner journey in a practical way.

The emphasis of both parts of the book is about the gradual blossoming and uncovering of the warm, bright, loving intelligence within each of us.

Handbook For Humans

560 pages, $16.95

"New cars have one, now so do humans"

SAUSALITO, Calif.—"If I have a talent, it is being able to learn almost any subject and present it clearly, without oversimplifying it or distorting it," James Sloman tells me.

I had complimented Sloman on his skill in integrating ideas from many spiritual sources in his book, *Handbook for Humans.*

Sloman is known in financial circles for his work on the Delta Phenomenon and the Adam Theory, which apply to trading systems. He was a stockbroker in Miami, a futures trader in Chicago and a market theorist in San Diego.

He started a book on markets more than eight years ago but put it aside when he felt directed to prepare the *Handbook.*

"I didn't know writing the *Handbook* would take so long," he said, but readers will not be surprised because his book is so thoroughly researched, from Taoism to diets, from evolution to empathy.

Sloman said we get handbooks when we buy cars and instructions when we buy appliances. Why shouldn't we benefit from a book of basic information for living?

The book's four parts—spirit, mind, heart and body—are each presented in "inner" and "outer" dimensions, resulting in eight principles: awareness, surrender, creation, production, equanimity, appreciation, simplicity and compassion. I asked him about the multitude of spiritual paths available today.

"All of them are potentially fruitful. The real test of one's own path is whether it leads to more open-heartedness in one's daily life," Sloman said. Sloman's book is available through Rayve Productions, (800) 852-4890.

—Vern Barnett, *Kansas City Star*

"If there were only one book..."

"If there were only one book you could read to navigate your way on the path of life, *Handbook for Humans* would be the perfect choice.

"Jimmy Sloman has created a treasure trove of wisdom from his personal experience and research...

"It's an outstanding, resourceful book with down-to-earth advice and information that feeds the soul and body. I am grateful for this book."

—Susan Smith Jones, author of
Choose to Live Peacefully

"A wonderful new book..."

"A wonderful new book by Jimmy Sloman is the manual he wishes he had received when he was growing up. *Handbook for Humans* is the culmination of a lifetime of learning and eight years of writing.

"In it, the author distills the wisdom of dozens of traditional paths to health, happiness, success and peace into an easy-to-digest overview of how our lives really work. *Handbook for Humans* succeeds as an excellent guide to help us achieve balance, equanimity, vibrancy and wholeness in our lives.

"The book is divided into four major sections addressing the spirit, mind, heart and body. Each section is then further divided into two parts, focusing on the inner dimension and then the outer dimension of each section.

"This format is terrific, as it allows the reader to understand what changes might be called for in his inner life to affect the outer manifestation he is seeking day-to-day...

"Peppered with dozens of real-life stories along with fables, folk tales, quotes & studies, *Handbook for Humans* is interesting to read as well as a course in what works.

"We recommend it highly."

—Patti Breitman, *EarthSave Marin*

Nothing

Hardback, 200 pages, $13.95

Nothing is a mind-mirror.

If we're making a frown but we're not aware of it, simply by looking in a mirror our face relaxes. Not that we do anything; our face relaxes simply from our becoming more aware of the situation.

A facial mirror will do for our face, but what about the frowns in our mind? *Nothing* holds up a mirror for the mind so that we can begin to look at it. And in that looking, a different perspective can arise in which our life is experienced in a different light.

"*Nothing* says it all and says it dead on...a masterwork. Thank you very, very much."

—D.T., Santa Barbara, CA

"I want to thank you for *Nothing*....I was truly moved and changed by reading this book. I have been on the path for a number of years reading all kinds of books, and *Nothing* is the best...truly beyond words."

—S.G., Phoenix, AZ

"Thank you for bringing into my life a book that I know is going to make a difference...the rest of my life."

—C.M., North Carolina

The Ripple

A novel, trade paper, $14.95

"*The Ripple,* written by James Sloman, author of the self-help manual *Handbook for Humans,* shows the broad range of Mr. Sloman's prodigious talent. Set in the overpowering environment of New York City in the 1970's (when it was written), *The Ripple* chronicles the breakdown of the human psyche as it strives for autonomy and recognition against the metropolis' spiraling whirlpool of anonymity and powerlessness.

"Sloman creates a darkly tragic yet humorous world where rage and regret dance a tango of bittersweet promise resigned to inevitable defeat. Punkin Miller, a computer programmer who is tormented by fellow workers, shop keepers and women beyond his means, reaches a breaking point...The result is a horrific, heartbreaking and mesmerizing ride as the reader follows Punkin Miller through the maze of mental meltdown, cat and mouse intrigue, and finally, total surrender to the crashing permanence of fate.

"As with *Handbook for Humans,* there are valuable lessons to be learned from *The Ripple* about the human condition. But make no mistake. *The Ripple* is a dark journey through the underside of the beast, and though redemption is found at last, the price is the loss of a soul."

—Michael Gottlieb, author of *Squeeze Play*

Songs From The Bottom Of The Sea

15 original songs, 3 covers; voice & guitar
Set of 2 CDs, $21.95

"Jackpot!"

"Now, perhaps more than ever, it seems that you can't swing a Martin steel-string without hitting a folk singer. But one of the great things about the persistence and popularity of singer-songwriter types is that every so often a new voice comes along that reminds us that folk singers can still be legit and likeable even in the '90s.

"In the vast sea of singer/songwriters, Sloman's rich, clear, well-recorded voice stands out in front of his songs..

"There's plenty here for folkies and non-folk fans alike to grab. In addition to his use of abundantly vivid personal details and storytelling/songwriting tactics ("Charlie"), Sloman's most surprising trick could be his rewrites of cover songs like "The Night They Drove Old Dixie Down" or "Summertime," where he gets the words down right but embellishes and distends the music, adding his own melody underneath to create a completely new song that's respectful and appreciative of the original, but fresh and vital nonetheless."

—*CMJ New Music Report*

Affecting Our Reality

An *extended* talk on 4 audio-cassettes
Galvin Auditorium, Chicago, $21.95

Topics of Discussion:

- Creative visioning
- The role of play in manifesting
- Looking at what's real
- Loving & accepting ourselves more
- The freedom of surrender
- The paradox of feelings
- Everything as a gift
- Life as mystery and magic

"A kind and soothing voice...I felt a sense of self-awareness, a warmth, a glow, a knowledge I've known before only I don't know where...a real insight to life and living."

—S.K., Miami, FL

"Thank you...wonderful!"

—J.M., St. Louis, MO

"So good...excellent!"

—C.C., Monterey, CA

TO ORDER BY TELEPHONE

VISA-MC-AMEX-DISCOVER

(800) 852-4890 (U.S., 24 hours)

(707) 838-6200 (abroad, 9-5 PST)

DISCOUNT SCHEDULE

2-4 total quantity	20%
5-9	25%
10-24	30%
25-99	35%
100+	40%

Prices are subject to change. Discounts apply to any mix of products.

SHIPPING & HANDLING

In the U.S., shipping is $3 per shipment plus $.95 for each item shipped. Express or international, please call for shipping.

MAY YOU BE HAPPY booklet

A booklet of excerpts from the book *May You Be Happy* is available from OceanBlue Publishing for the cost of shipping (and a donation if you like).

Order Form

YourName ______________________

StreetAddress ______________________

CityStateZip ______________________

Telephone ______________________

	QUANTITY	PRICE	AMOUNT
May You Be Happy		$11.95	
Handbook for Humans		$16.95	
Nothing		$13.95	
The Ripple		$14.95	
Songs From... Sea set		$21.95	
Affecting Our Reality set		$21.95	
TOTAL QUANTITY (FOR DISCOUNT)			
AMOUNT SUM			
Subtract Discount (see opposite page)			
SUBTOTAL			
SalesTax (CA residents add 7.5%)			
Shipping (see opposite page)			
TOTAL ENCLOSED			

PLEASE SEND YOUR ORDER TO:

OceanBlue Publishing
98 Main Street
Tiburon, CA 94920